A
LIBRARY PARTNERS PRESS
AWARD WINNER

Gail O'Day

POETRY AWARD

2018

Let Go or Hold Fast

Beaufort Poems

For Kate

Susan

ALSO BY SUSAN SCHMIDT

Landfall Along the Chesapeake,
In the Wake of Captain John Smith

Salt Runs in My Blood

Song of Moving Water

LET GO OR HOLD FAST

BEAUFORT POEMS

Susan Schmidt

library partners press

a digital publishing imprint

A Library Partners Press Award Winner, 2018
First Edition, First Printing

Copyright © 2019 Susan Schmidt

Front cover photo courtesy of Kevin B. Moore
Author photo by Marge Terhaar
Page design by Tim Durning/Scribe Inc.

TEXT Warnock Pro Regular
DISPLAY FreightNeo Pro

Library of Congress Cataloging-in-Publication Data
Schmidt, Susan, 1949–
    Let go or hold fast / Susan Schmidt.
p. cm.
ISBN 978-1-61846-066-0 (alk. paper)
1. North Carolina—Poetry
2. Southern States—Poetry
I. Title
PS3568.A6

Produced and Distributed By:
Library Partners Press
ZSR Library
Wake Forest University
1834 Wake Forest Road
Winston-Salem, North Carolina 27106

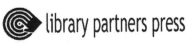

www.librarypartnerspress.org
Manufactured in the United States of America

FOR

Science, Endangered Species
Migratory Bird Treaty Act
Clean Water, Clear Air, Wilderness
Neighbors

The cure for anything is salt water: sweat, tears or the sea.
—Isak Dinesen

Fish, amphibian, and reptile, warm-blooded bird, and mammal—
each of us carries in our veins a salty stream in almost the same
proportions as in sea water.
—Rachel Carson

Over the last sixty years, the world population of seabirds has
dropped by over two-thirds. One-third of all seabird species is
now threatened with extinction. We have brought this disaster on
ourselves: through overfishing; by the massive accidental catching
of birds in fishing gear; by introducing rats, cats, dogs to the
breeding sites of birds; through pollution by oil, metals, plastics;
destruction of nesting sites; and through the multiple effects of
climate change and acidification of the sea.
—Adam Nicolson

Contents

BREEZE

Beaufort Scale Force 2–6

HIGH TIME

On the sand I pick up shells
with a hundred eroded holes.
Orrin Pilkey says shells may be
ten to twenty thousand years old,
rolled up from the ancient seabed
and tumbled to the shore.
It's only a matter of time.

The west point of Shackleford has eroded
almost a mile in four years from augur
dredging the channel to Morehead Port.
The west end of Bird Shoal is moving north
twelve feet a year, exposing Beaufort
to a direct hit of the next hurricane.

Within the last hundred thousand years,
Stan Riggs says the oceanfront has moved
forty miles inland or forty miles
offshore. The satellite photo of
eastern North Carolina shows
the distinct drop-off of the
Suffolk Scarp. Along Highway 17
north of Williamston, you can
clearly see the old beachfront dune.
Not if but when
we're under water again.
It's only a matter of time.

SUCH GRACE

Terns nest on the beach spit
south of First Deep Creek
a foot or two from high tide.
A nest is shallow like my hand,
the egg camouflaged
the color of sand.

Having rowed hard
against wind and tide,
I drift down the creek,
free ride, pushed home
by tide and wind,
to the landing.

At dusk
black-capped, sharp-winged
least terns weave lace,
dart and turn like bobbins,
grazing no-see-ums that bite
tender skin on my wrists.

As I watch the sun drop west,
curved-bill ibis,
black-legged egrets
wing east down Taylors Creek
to roost before dark.

RISING ANXIETY

Rising sea level closes
stormwater drains so heavy rains
flood ditches and intersections.

As groundwater approaches
the surface of my land
a block from the creek

I can feel the ground swell and fall
in waves like jumping on a
sphagnum-moss bog.

When I ask Pat the tire guy if
my car needs aligning, he says,
"You live in Beaufort, don't you?"

No point filling potholes.
Asphalt can't hold its shape
on undulating earth.

Where grass grows in dirt holes
in my road I do consider
planting Begonias.

On Cedar Street and Ann Street
I slalom around potholes
like a Class-3 river rapid

or the chop set up
in the creek
when wind opposes tide.

A mile from the ocean inlet
water is rising under us.
Are foundations cracking yet?

2016/ 1970/ 1670

Wistful I climb to the sun
above mist and fog.
When I was young
I would stride
straight uphill
to the clouds.

I pause in the wind
and look out to sea.
On my twenty-first
I climbed Snowdon
three hundred years after
my Quaker ancestor left Northern Wales.

The mountain's copper, coal
profit lies underground
but I could never
work in the dark.
The summit to me means
being closer to the sky.

Descending I traverse
steep bluebell slopes
as I read slant-slab orogeny.
Layer-cake rocks speak Welsh
named after tribes—
Cambrian Ordovician Silurian.

In the high pasture
fat lambs butt mamas' bellies.
Here, with a view of the estuary—
did Job Meredith live
in these stone walls?
—thatch roof long gone.

Below in the forest
I feel doubly at home
recognizing tree species.
On the beach I pick stones
worn so smooth white veins
show their structure.

As I sleep at sea level like at home
each wave rolls the stones
and lambs baa all night long.

1

I dream trouble is coming.

From my office, one person motors
out to sea in an inflatable dinghy
to meet the danger, head on.

A second person in a dark room
with a wall of blinking red lights
is monitoring the magnitude of the threat.

I walk the beach, in silence, impatient,
waiting to learn my assignment.

When I tell the dream in House Church,
Bennett the Bishop says, "That is your work.
In a dream, all three characters are you."

2

In a dream I hold a ball in my palm:
the Earth, blue and green as seen from space,
the size and pliant like a loggerhead egg, and
as fragile. Have you ever held a sea turtle egg?
Soft and leathery, easy to squeeze.

It is my job to witness—water, birds.
Wind, sand, and stars. On a dark night
full of stars, decades ago, in a full gale
on a sailboat at sea, I sang Christmas carols
for peace, oceans, and species.

To keep the planet company, to give it strength
to keep rolling, make anything creative—bread,
pottery, poetry, painting, music, gardens. I row
the creek, paddle the marsh in silence or singing.

Barefoot I walk the beach so my feet no longer
fit in closed-toe shoes. Yoga toes! Sun
behind me casts my shadow tall and skinny.

SAFE DARK

Downtown I can find friends to dance with
in my small town. When the electricity blinks
off, Aqua restaurant provides candles. Kim
says, "Pay close enough. No cash register."

Walking home, the whole town is dark.
No streetlights, no porch lights.
A mile in star-shine and moon-glow,
Front Street like a private driveway.

No buzz of heat pumps or TV.
Warm enough sea breeze.
No car headlights. Just
the hum of surf in the Inlet.

Black-crowned night herons perch
on pilings. Tide laps on yachts
at docks. Rigging rattles on sailboats
moored in the creek. I remember

a midnight, when I swirled, safe, middle of
dark Ann Street, after flying back from
Africa. I wouldn't live in Kenya, where we
barricaded inside a wall with an armed guard.

ROWING FORWARD, FACING BACKWARD

Spartina grass is new spring-green.
Mating season, red-wing blackbirds
claim territory on myrtle and yaupon
with shrill trills. Triplets of swallows
hover and dip. On stilts, great egrets
wade by oysters and red-billed
oystercatchers on vast sand flats
exposed at low tide.

I row the tidal creek, open at both ends
between Gallants Channel and white
phosphate domes at Morehead Port.
Right here the State wants to sink
pilings in the marsh for a high bridge
to move tractor-trailer trucks faster
to the Port. Small town, no rush,
I don't mind waiting for the
old drawbridge to open or close.

I skim over shallows, facing backward.
The sliding-seat shell I row draws scant
inches. In skinny water I float light and
fast. If I run aground, I won't step
out or I'd sink thigh deep into muck.
If I drag the boat, oyster shells would
lacerate my ankles and scrape the race-
slick hull. Instead, I can wait an hour
for the tide to rise, watching
a lone blue heron watch the water.

NEVER ASK FOR A TOW

I am the same age as my father
when he died, forty years ago.
Dare hope I'm in better shape.

A few months before his heart attack,
I rig the sailboat he keeps to lure me
home to the Bay. Helping him step
from the dock to the boat, I sense
how frail and unstable he is. Holding
the tiller, though mostly blind, he feels
the wind on his nose and steers true,
cutting through smooth blue waves,
blue sky. I handle main and jib sheets,
as my father gives me cues, "Ready
About" that he's tacking, "Hard Alee."
He taught me to sail as a girl, and
now I am enabling his best pleasure.

Overnight, land is cooler than water
until sun warms the land surface.
Midday we are becalmed offshore,
quiet and content, quite a while, in the lull
between the morning breeze that blows
from land to water and the afternoon
breeze that blows from water to land.
Finite time floating together, but I must
drive three hours to teach in Charlottesville.
Despite knowing my father's reluctance, I hail
a neighbor's motorboat to tow us in. Chagrin.
A Chesapeake sailor never asks for a tow.

CONSERVING ENERGY

Hanging laundry is meditative and saves
energy. I check the forecast and may wait
five days for the sun. Sheets and towels
will smell like fresh air. Drape and hook
with old wood clothespins. Like Delft,
dishtowels are blue and white.

Lean over and pull chickweed from
Liriope beds underfoot, daydream.
On a crisp day, low humidity, no bugs,
I say wishfully, "It's always like this."
Afraid August and September will be
as hot as January was cold. Extremes.

Kiwi the dog drops a red ball in the laundry
basket for me to throw under the live oak.
Sixteen-foot-diameter trunk, wide high canopy.
Why I bought this house. Imagine druids.
I love you, tree, but how much longer are you
dropping pollen on porch cushions and dry
brown catkins that the dog tracks in the house?
After twenty inches of rain last year, runoff
from weekend neighbor's driveway gouged
a gulley in the backyard. St. Augustine Turf
designed for the shade is filling in lush green.

A bird is singing "hurdy-gurdy, hurdy-gurdy."
I drape and pin socks and jeans. My clothes
are mostly grape, blueberry, periwinkle.
Hang shirts on hangers; I never iron.
Laundry is my slowest calming chore. Until
I walk into the kitchen and smell oatmeal
burning the new pan on the stove I forgot
to turn off. In the right state of mind,
washing dishes is also a meditative practice.

OUR ROSE

Forty years ago, the stained menu at Sinbad's
waterfront café said, "Beaufort, Jumping-Off
Place to the Islands and the World." Before
tourists, "coolest small town" and paid parking
meters, the first folks who moved here were
fishermen, marine scientists, and sailboat cruisers.
Back then, the waterfront was ragged with piers
for commercial fishing boats, bait shops,
Barbour's Marine. Then, a federal grant built the
two-block yacht dock. Because insurance companies
do not cover boats to sail dangerous shoals around
Hatteras, they ride the Intracoastal Waterway south
from Norfolk then "jump off" into the Atlantic.

Rowing The Cut, I float to the stern
of *Our Rose*, a 44-foot catamaran with a
Commonwealth flag. "Where y'all from?"
"New Zealand." "Yes, I know;
where are you from?" "North Island."
They admire my dog. "Meet Kiwi."
They go wild. "Come aboard for tea."

Every year I ask one boat, "Do you need
a shower, laundry, ride to the grocery?" But
their boat has a water-maker, washing machine.
"What Jennifer does need is an X-ray." She slipped
on an icy dock in Hampton and can't find a doctor
to see her. I call my orthopedic surgeon, whose son
is sailing around the world. Good news: Just strained,
not broken. I read the blog as *Our Rose* parties
in the Caribbean, overwinters in Guatemala,
crosses the Panama Canal and the Pacific to
Papua New Guinea, Indonesia, and Thailand.
Our Rose now sits for sale in Malaysia. From
my small town I imagine the Far East.

DROUGHT

I am a gardener
in a season of drought.
I can see the black cloud
twenty miles north
raining on the Neuse River.
The weatherman predicts
forty-percent chance rain
though none falls here.

Thirsty like my plants
I wake to the sound of water
by my window
sluicing the gutter downspout
to the empty water tank
to hoses that will soak
seedlings next week.

Raindrops plinking
on live oak leaves
and my neighbor's tin roof.
After a dry spring
hard soil wants
a gentle approach.

Just when I rise
the drizzle stops
too soon, hardly enough
to store in cisterns
for tomorrow.

UNTIL THE NEW BRIDGE
TRIPLES THE DISTANCE

Kiwi, my little brown water spaniel, runs
loose on Radio Island, beyond where
babies dig in the sand and splash in shallows—
until the new high bridge triples the distance.
We walk the beach at low tide. No birds
nest here. Because of erosion, high tide
covers the sand to the scruff woods. A fox
on the beach fearless before dusk, rumors of
coyotes. Kiwi retrieves a rubber stick I toss
in the channel twenty times. Until the express
ferry carrying tourists to Shackleford throws
huge wakes in the No-Wake Zone. I used
to swim here more at incoming high tide.
But three new marinas upstream raise bacteria
at this swimming park. Wakes from the ferry
erode the beach and endanger babies,
my wet dog Kiwi and me.

On Radio Island beach, with my brown dog,
I find a green turtle, perfect except quite dead.
I carry it, twenty pounds, slightly stinky,
down the beach half a mile and roll it in plastic
to transport to Matt, the state turtle scientist.
The turtle is three to five years old, he says.
All grown, the turtle would have weighed
four hundred pounds. From barnacles
on his shell, he was too weak to dive to feed.
Probably stunned in a January cold snap.

NOT ALL TOURISTS ARE DITDOTS

Trash on the public beach at Radio Island:
Cigarette butts, cigarette boxes, beer cans, beer bottles:
      a dozen butts next to a dozen beer cans.
Plastic water bottles, plastic toys, straws.
Empty bait boxes, full boxes redolent of dead shrimp,
      fishing line, hooks and rubber worms.
Fast-food wrappers, Styrofoam thrown into marshgrass.
Walmart price tags ripped from chairs, umbrellas, rafts;
broken umbrella, broken chair, deflated raft left behind:
      Umbrella poles I tote home stake beans in my garden.
By the parking-lot toilet-house, a full diaper
on the concrete under the outdoor shower.
The showerhead is stolen, again, already.
Only May, beginning of the tourist season.

Ditdots are a bit worse than dingbatters.
Weekend People, who drive 70 miles an hour
from Raleigh, drive 50 miles an hour on Ann Street's
25-mile-an-hour zone—where children, dogs, bikes,
pedestrians should have right of way. I don't take out
my kayak on three-day weekends when speed-freaks
in motorboats throw mindless wakes. One joyrider
zooms into the creek without looking left, right, or
straight-ahead; barely misses ramming Julian's sloop
under sail. Two more high-rise storage sheds
for 467 motorboats are permitted
on the banks of Taylors Creek.

DWELL IN SAFETY

My town juts into the ocean thirty miles from the Gulf Stream.
Why do you live willingly in the path of hurricanes? someone
upstate asks. I say with faith—No place is safer than the beach
to face wind and water, because high tide ebbs back to sea.

Isabel approaches the coast blowing 150 miles an hour,
which would knock Beaufort flat, force growing
exponentially with speed. As the barometer drops, I haul
the boat from the dock, move porch chairs to the shed.
Heartsick I say, "Not here. Hit someplace else, please."

The scary part is waiting. Afraid to be stranded
on a highway, I stay put alone in my dark house,
plywood boarding windows. Nine feet above sea level,
ants march inside as water rises a block away. At the eye,
at the depth of low pressure, my old broken bones ache—
ribs and wrist. I sleep deep, air sucked out of my lungs.

On the Outer Banks, folks would tie themselves to trees
in case the house floated away. Isabel lands twelve miles east,
crosses Core Sound, hits Davis and Stacy at 110 with a wall
of water ten feet high, five feet deep in two hundred homes.

After flood tide recedes, I help scrub mud Downeast.
By the road are refrigerators, mustard-plaid sofas,
FEMA numbers sprayed on trees, carpets ripped
out but mildew in floors and walls forever.

"Deflect, deflect," I'd said. But no place is safe.
Hurricanes go where they want. When I ask
for fear and pain and loss to steer clear,
the storm may hit my neighbor. I should ask
instead for grace to handle whatever happens.

HOW PINK

In the first house I bought as a teacher,
I painted the fireplace mantel
a rosy pink that matched
the inside of a queen conch shell
I collected sailing in the Bahamas.

I paint my Beaufort house pink
like all nine houses on Gun Cay,
a tiny island on the Florida Straits
between Lauderdale and Nassau.
Like one house on Portsmouth Island
by Ocracoke Inlet, because the
mailboat delivered one can of red
and one can of white paint.

Not Pepto-Bismol, peach, apricot,
cherry, salmon, cotton candy, coral,
a cartoon piglet or frou-frou dyed poodle.

Pale pink. Jean Toomer in *Cane*
compared a lady's complexion
to the eastern horizon at sunset.
I worship sunsets, good as any religion.
What better use of an afternoon
than to wait on the waterfront
and stare at the sky for flaming streaks
of magenta reflected in the creek
or faded blushing hues.

Considering what color to paint these
dining room walls, peeling badly, not
scraped or sanded for thirty-eight years—
I want a white in the lightest shade of pink
to match Audubon's flamingo print,
Dhurrie rugs and dragon-fruit venetian blinds.

A Japonica camellia by the front porch,
blooming at Solstice after the first frost,
is cheery pink like the house outside.
The ragged edge of the petal is pastel,
contemplative white I want for walls inside.
Like the pink and white Roseate Spoonbill
that strayed from Key West to Bird Shoal.

ARIEL'S SONG

Walking Bird Shoal
   in high-pressure calm
      that follows a nor-easter
a strange shape mars the sand flat.
    A huge buoy, my height and more,
blown from the storm, its anchor chain broken,
     iron links, five inches, the width of my hand span,
       marking my safe shore:
             "Do Not Anchor
Do Not Approach within 300 feet."

At sea I'd have to sail within a boat-length
   to read the fine print.
              Nearsighted
I navigate close to danger to learn from
   the experience.

Did high wind break the cable and
     blow the float ashore?
In last night's storm-tide was
      the buoy's flotation stronger than its foothold?
     Released from under water
       ghost-depths of old sailors.
  "Full fathom five my father lies."

How strong are shackles
   to friends, to place, to life?
As I search for harbor
     with no chart or compass,
how do I heed the buoy's warning?
     Do Not Approach
     Do Not Anchor
Does that mean to let go or hold fast?

II GALE

Beaufort Scale Force 7–9

SMILING SECRETS

Dolphins rise to the surface
to breathe, lucky them
to enjoy both water and air.

I envy their two kingdoms
as each season sea level
rises visibly in The Cut.

In Gallants Channel three adults
herd eight rolling, leaping juveniles
to a cove away from boat motors.

On the Museum's boat *Spyhop* I call directions
from the bow, nine o'clock and two o'clock,
and point for Keith to photograph them.

Cetacean scientist, he can identify
every dolphin's dorsal fin, summer/
winter residents, spring/ fall migrants.

Out the Inlet in front of Shackleford,
we follow three feeding dolphins
then four, then five to Lookout Bight.

Sleek slippery silver, do dolphins
jump just for fun? Frolic, since
they are smarter than we are.

Down they dive to feed
for a minute then surface
to breathe and leap again.

They're smiling, sad, resilient
as if keeping secrets of survival
we humans should learn.

HOW TO GET RID OF SWEET ANTS

Beaufort is an anthill. One scientist estimates
several trillion. When Front Street floods,
ants crowd my house on high ground.

Ants swarm when I dig in my garden.
Like a good Buddhist,
I gently ask ants to leave;
       they don't listen.

Hang the hummingbird feeder between two lines
of monofilament. Ants still fill the feeder.
Pour hot water, gas, vinegar in their holes;
       it doesn't work.

Mix Borax detergent half and half with sugar.
Spread Splenda around the house foundation
       (fake sugar kills us too, eventually).

Sprinkle Baby Powder to confuse ants
so they lose their scent trail (but
       don't let your baby eat the stuff).

At doorways, scatter Cayenne Pepper and
Bay Leaves. Draw chalk lines at windowsills;
ants don't like sticky feet.
       They come in anyway.

Dump Diatomaceous Earth behind kitchen
drawers; dubious if safe for pets and kids.
Spray White Vinegar;
       it's acid, not poison.

Cover counters with Peppermint.
Tea Tree Oil, Citronella, costly Lavender.
The ant parade will smell like a spa.

Toss all food scraps in a big glass jar,
never in the trash can. Then empty it
into the compost bin in the front yard—
    Where ants will multiply.

COURTING PLUMAGE

One April morning, light wind,
no motorboats, no wake or whitecaps.
I paddle through Deep Creek to Bird Shoal
and think, no better time than "flat cam."
I paddle two more miles across North River
to Middle Marsh and enter quiet shallow creeks
to the cedar hammock, where I see first twenty,
then sixty, then a hundred orange-bill, all-white
great egrets in fluffy breeding plumage.
Males take turns jumping to a top branch and
stretch their necks skyward to attract the ladies.
All of them: white wings rolled back and fringed-
feather "nuptial aigrettes" blowing in the breeze.
How soon till they diminish or disappear?

BIRD WATCHING

1

On Bird Shoal on my monthly dead-shorebird survey,
at the western end is a loon with its head torn off
by a diving osprey. At the eastern spit I find
a banded royal tern lying peacefully, as if asleep.
It was banded before it fledged from this same beach
twenty-five years ago—a good flight. I did hear
of a royal tern that lived thirty-one years.

2

I paddle with a weekend guest but tell her
we should be off Taylors Creek by Sunday noon.
At high tide, we cut through Deep Creek to Bird Shoal.
Extra high tide after a storm, so terns and sandpipers,
plovers, skimmers and oystercatchers congregate
on the beach spit. We float silently by bird clans
in our kayaks till 11:30. Then four Sunday speedboats
roar in and drop anchor; unload chairs, beer coolers,
radios blaring rock and roll. Four happy black Labs
jump out and poop, chase and scatter shy shorebirds
clustered on the spit. I approach each motorboat
picnic and quietly ask them to leash their dogs,
"This island is the Rachel Carson Reserve."
"Who are You?"

   As Nature Conservancy steward, thirty-eight years ago,
   I wrote rules to protect the birds and the grant
   for the State to buy Carrot Island and Bird Shoal.
Who me? "I'm a bird warden."

FEATHERY ABUNDANCE

*This is one of the ages of loss. Seabirds are
keeping watch at the gates of extinction.*

ADAM NICOLSON

With State Wildlife biologists, I count five thousand
shorebird nests on a dredge-spoil island near the
Lighthouse. White ibis, great egret, cattle egret,
one snowy egret. Great blue heron, little blue heron,
tricolor heron. What privilege to witness so much
feathery abundance this sunny cool May morning.

We're about to get hot. In a line, we bushwhack
five hours through thickets, duck under branches,
briars and vines; and stop, bushed, to drink water.
I'm two or three times the age of the paid bird-crew.
In stick nests, squirming naked ibis hatch from
splotched buff-blue eggs. Perched nearby,
curved-red-bill adults growl at us. Both
parents take turns feeding young.

North of the berm, nests are full of new chicks.
Baby egrets are scruffy white, clumsy; their
cracked eggs green-blue. If I bump, or one
jumps out, I must replace it as a mother will
ignore a chick on the ground. In a black-crowned
night heron nest, a hefty gray four-inch chick,
as big as the other two, barks at me.

On the beach, we avoid stepping on greenish
gull eggs and mottled-tan tern eggs in palm-size
depressions and will return next week to count
them. We wear wading shoes to cross the shoals,
but no leg protection. For three days, I gouge
twenty thorns out of each shredded ankle,
but am grateful thousands of chicks
will fledge and forage on Bird Shoal.

MOTHER'S DAY

Southwest prevailing wind 14 knots
pushes my Whitehall rowboat against
slack-high ebbing tide. Kiwi and I are
floating east in The Cut, 30 feet north
of the beach, silent, watching ibis, egrets,
curlews feeding, wet feet, in the marshes.

A motorboat just north of us is also floating,
respectful, watching the week-old pony
that prances on the sand by the creek
with his mother just two feet behind,
and two more mares plodding sentinels.

A loud-laughing speedboat blaring music,
kicking a high wake 8 a.m. Sunday morning.
Girls in bikinis already in May see the pony.
It turns a tight circle suddenly, throwing a wave
that rocks my rowboat, and drives straight fast
to the beach, terrifying the horses that clamber
into the scrub woods, the mother and two aunts
pushing the baby up a steep four-foot berm.
Really?

I must balance splendid natural neighbors
with my disdain for ditdots, local term for
tourists. Rearranged letters mean idiots.

GREEN THOUGHT IN GREEN SHADE

annihilating all that's made

ANDREW MARVELL

We have lost their laughing color in the sky,
the only wild parrot this far north,
lost because honeybees filled their nests,
because we chopped down cypress swamps.

I count seven askew in Audubon's print by my bed:
life size, a foot long, leaf-green tail and wings,
yellow neck and scarlet cheeks, big black eyes
and curved beaks biting cockleburs.

When one bright parrot was shot:
the loud emerald flock would sink
and surround her, bewildered.
We humans rarely see such devotion.

Was it love? fearlessness or folly? For a hunter
could shoot a hundred more on the ground
and fill a burlap sack for the milliner
to adorn preening ladies' bonnets.

One gunman said, "Several shots fill a basket."
After shooting these seven to paint, Audubon
wrote: "The flesh is tolerable food. But,
kept as pets, they never learn to talk."

Shot for green fashion-feathers.
Shot because hundreds picked an orchard clean,
in fact bit to the core for the seeds and
spit out whole the white apple fruit.

The last died in the wild a hundred years ago.
The last one in a zoo soon after. What fun
would one bird have alone who
frolicked with such raucous company?

Women no longer wear feathered hats
but Carolina Parakeets are long gone
like the Ivory-Bill despite uncertain
flashes of vivid green through the trees.

WHERE WILD

A yellow-and-red corn snake,
looking for a new home, is curled
by my front door one morning.
"Shoo," I say. "The porch is mine
and my dog's. Go eat mice in the garden
and scare away cats that harass birds."
Two days later, I hear a neighbor squealing,
about to chop off my harmless corn snake's
head with a shovel. So I trap it in a five-gallon
bucket and drive it to the shrub thicket
on Radio Island. In the car, Li my Chinese
renter holds down the lid. The corn snake
wants to sunbathe on the road instead of
safe in the bushes. The photograph shows,
uncoiled, he's eight feet long.

LIKE A KANGAROO

Daybreak, Kiwi is barking over the edge
of the porch. A young possum, refugee,
hides under the rosemary bush. Hush,
Kiwi. Possums freeze when alarmed.
The swamp forest behind my house
was once full of turtles, frogs, snakes,
owls who fled when a developer clearcut
ten acres to build forty-two houses.
Before drainage ditches and mitigation
ponds there were few mosquitoes here.
Hawks and owls ate snakes; turtles and
snakes ate frogs; frogs ate dragonflies
that ate mosquitoes in the swamp.

My jungle garden is one patch of wildness
left in town. I am ashamed to be startled,
at first, by the little critter. America's
only marsupial. Pink nose, white snout,
gray back, perky ears. One possum can
eat an acre of ticks, four thousand ticks
a week. This guest eats cockroaches,
rats, garden slugs. Immune to venom,
possums can eat rattlesnakes.
Welcome, baby, please stay.

IRISH TATTOO

1
I don't need a tattoo. I'm Irish.
I have enough rusty freckles,
  though in no pattern or design.
Scars from bicycling gravel roads as a kid,
  bruises from moving too fast.
"Barnacles" from being fair skinned.

Red threads of varicose veins.
  When did I get my mother's legs?
These sturdy calves have walked
a thousand miles of Celtic coastal paths;
thick peasant ankles can dance all night.

Summer thorns gouged my ankles,
  too hot for pants or socks:
Counting egret nests on Davis Island.
Tagging Crystal Skipper butterflies
  in Fort Macon dunes.
Portaging forty downed trees
on Contentnea Creek: begrudging
  Hurricane Matthew.

2

At Wild Caught music festival, I stand
too long by my car digging for earplugs,
          Kayla channeling Janis Joplin.
Ouch, ouch, ouch! —I look down to see
I am standing on a fire-ant mound and
my feet in sandals have a dozen stings.
          (Is their poison cumulative?)
Under the Carteret Catch tent,
my face gets redder and my feet itchier.
I move an ice block from foot to foot.
Penny says, *My house **now** for drugs.*
Benadryl lightens my face and
hydrocortisone cools my feet.

          When the deluge comes,
I carry an umbrella to the food tent.
How many times this summer
          have I said *torrential*?
That night my ankles are bright blue:
blood poisoning my first thought.
Then I remember: my batik dress
is wet, bleeding below my knees.
I can wash the blue ink off my feet.

PREDATOR

I am swimming fifty feet offshore,
six o'clock, when a man comes running
up the beach, yelling, "Shark! Shark!"
I stroke ashore and walk south toward the shark.
Sporty fishermen are casting in light surf;
women sit under umbrellas reading paperbacks.
In the shallows I see a long black dart.

A small shark—black-tipped dorsal and fins—
that can grow max nine feet. I'm glad no
upstate redneck runs for a gun to shoot
the predator. Folks on the beach seem
to appreciate it. In mid-calf depth, before
dusk, the little shark is grazing on baitfish.

Swimming so shallow, it gets stuck
on the sand. A fisherman wades in and
pushes with his foot in a tennis shoe.
It does not budge, hard aground.
The man picks up the shark, cradling
it on each forearm. Two or three feet
drooping to his left and right.

The shark does not wiggle, nor turn to bite.
The man waddles to mid-thigh depth
and tosses the shark into deeper water.
Fast it shoots back to shore to feed.

MONARCHS

For one day in October
when pecans drop from the tree
by the field where my dog
chases tennis balls every morning
butterflies graze on
lavender-blue ageratum bushes.

Two years ago I saw eight Monarch
butterflies and last year just six.
But this year two dozen Monarchs
swill nectar from wispy bluish blooms.
Regal stain-glass orange and black
flutter and perch; paler dun
camouflage when wings fold.
Two days later only five butterflies
feed on blue ageratum, and then a day later
none. So maybe, other years I was a day
early or late to see twenty-four.

Thirty years ago thousands of Monarchs
filled my sail on a Chesapeake creek.
Three generations of Monarchs fly north
in spring to Canada, and the October batch
flies south three thousand miles all the way
to the Mexican mountain they've never seen.

Mourning their decline, I plant milkweed.
Broadcast seed won't grow.
Late winter, I must nurture seedlings in pots,
transplant early spring in my backyard plot
so migrating Monarchs can lay eggs here.
I blame industrial pesticides, *Neonicotinoids*
that kill honeybees, butterflies, and songbirds,
just as cigarette nicotine killed my mother.

TWILIGHT

1

Taut silver like mackerel skin,
tide slides out the creek. Smooth
mauve glow surrounds the horizon.

The stiff breeze all day has dropped
at dusk. A mile south surf still roars
on the front beach. The round full

moon is pale until the sky darkens.
East southeast the Lighthouse
blinks on every fifteen seconds.

This moment of calm on the dock,
grateful for bright constellations,
I watch Venus rise.

2

Wrens, cardinals, sparrows, blackbirds
spit out cheap wild seed in the yard.
After a hurricane's high water,

rats attracted to cracked corn chew
into heat ducts below my floor.
At dark when rats start to move,

I catch them through heat-vent holes
in black plastic snap traps tied to
fishing leader. They squeak one last

moment as I pull them up, small
wharf rats with long tails. New metal
ducts will cost four thousand dollars.

TOO LATE

In November, at a marina on the creek
the dock crew has draped hoses over
the wall for two manatees who guzzle
water. Gentle gray-rubber giants, both
with prop scars. Closest kin on earth
is the elephant. They eat plants, either
salt or fresh, and need to drink fresh
water. Giving manatees any food or
water, though kind, is illegal. Everywhere
they're endangered. In Florida, they cluster
at power-plant outflows. They can't survive
water colder than sixty degrees. This late
in the year, no manatee has survived
so far north. I lie flat, close as I can. Tell
them, "Leave. Leave now. Go south. Fast."

HOW TO SURVIVE A BEE ATTACK

Be calm. Exude no perfume
that attracts bees to pollinate.
No pheromone that suggests mating.
No sweat to induce anger. Forget
the ten thousand bees on your arms
and knees. Think polar cool. Chew
gum but don't move your lips.
Don't flutter your eyelids.
Hope a breeze will blow them away
or waft the scent of a tupelo
blossom in the next woodlot.
Count your blessings, slowly
one to a hundred.
One bee sting is good for arthritis.
Two bee stings good for character.
Three bee stings build resistance.
Think pollination, almonds,
apples. Think gratitude.

SWIMMING IN A METEOR SHOWER

Early October in Beaufort the first cold
northeast wind is called the mullet blow
when fish born in marshes swim out the Inlet
for two years at sea. Wading birds, surf-rods,
and gill nets wait to catch the rush of fish.

I avoid swimming when sharks feed at dusk
and dawn. The water at Radio Island is
cleaner at incoming tide—shrimp docks
and live-aboard boats upstream.
Noon, I wade in, immerse, float,
stroke, and turn my neck to breathe.

Suddenly
I'm swimming into light
like a meteor shower.
Inch-long silversides stream around me,
silver stripes painted on clear bodies.
I feel luminous, but stand thigh deep
when I remember bluefish
with sharp teeth chase smaller fry.

In the sky: hundreds of black skimmers
roll in a wave like shaking dust
from a quilt. I figure they undulate
for fun after eating their fill of fish.
As they bank in synchrony
their color changes—
black backs, white bellies and
underwings catch the light.

IIII STORM

Beaufort Scale Force 10–11

TYRANNY OF SMALL DECISIONS

I am stunned by a vast clearcut of swamp forest
down the road behind my house. I dreaded it coming,
but not this bad: Not one tree left standing on
a hundred acres where I used to see a mystery of trees.

Mega-ton dumptrucks filled with dirt send
shock waves when they speed past, so no more
cycling that quiet road. Our Town won't fill more
potholes; taxes must pay for new fire trucks.

I hear that a baby bear was running scared
down a nearby street, its home and mama lost.
I had no idea bears lived so close. Then they
bulldoze a hundred more acres next to marsh.

I live with a small brown dog who resembles a bear.
I grew up reading *Winnie the Pooh*, cuddling toy bears
named after Teddy Roosevelt who created national parks.
In pleas to save wild land, photos of baby bears torment me.

When Beaufort Town Board approved almost 800 houses
on 200 acres, I protested loss of habitat for owls, hawks, snakes,
raccoons, possums, foxes, which can all live in my backyard.
I had no idea bears lived here. Each bear needs forty-five acres.

I protested loss of oxygen we breathe from
chopping down trees, release of carbon into
our hotter world, loss of swamp-forest sponge
to keep Beaufort from flooding as sea level rises.

My professor Bill Odum talked about small decisions
that create big problems—when easy, greedy choices
accumulate irrevocably. No bureaucracy
asks us first before they sell out the wetlands.

NO HOME NO PREY

When I cycle home from Sunday School,
a police car is parked in a neighbor's yard.
I poke my head behind her house and ask,
"Okay?" Man in blue says, "We have an owl."

There in the grass sits a little owl with ear tufts,
gray-brown, white on his throat, reddish brown
face, barred underparts. A juvenile puffed up
to double his size. Great Horned Owl.

"On the ground half an hour," timid neighbor says.
"I heard it thunk my porch. Called the cop."
The downed owl rotates his head, blinks
his yellow eyes with big black iris, alert.

I sit on the grass sixteen feet from the owl and
mumble to calm him. Hunting in the sunshine,
day-blind he has stunned himself. Evicted when
200 acres of woods down the road were bulldozed.

"No one can touch an endangered bird without
federal permit," Officer Ginther says. "The wildlife
shelter will take him but won't transport." I phone
Josh who has a marine-mammal permit.

I babble to the dandy owl and wave away
a taunting mockingbird. Still hungry, the owl hops
to my canvas bag. Sharp beak, long curved talons.
Then bounces ten feet into a crepe myrtle bush.

Josh arrives with leather gloves. Next door
I gather dog crate, shower curtains, more gloves.
As three of us approach the owl, his cheek feathers
compress, skinny and scared, just a little guy.

As Josh is about to pounce from behind to wrap him,
he suddenly flies to a tree branch forty feet high,
wings spread wide! "Best possible outcome."
I watch the young owl till he disappears, homeless.

HOW HIGH ARE YOU?

My friend Bev who lives in Montana
at five thousand feet asks me, "How much
longer are you going to live there?"
Where else, I ask, can I play in boats
year round? Cleanest air in the world,
and lots of air when the wind blows.
She means sea-level rise, being at risk
in the path of hurricanes that ride
the Gulf Stream, and State Legislature
elected by gerrymandering hell-bent
to gut environmental protection.

From Terry Joyce, ocean-current scientist
at Woods Hole, I learn the AMOC,*
conveyor belt that carries cold water south
and warm water north, is slowing,
which will speed climate change.

Terry lives uphill on Cape Cod
thirty feet above sea level.
He asks me, "How high do you live?"
"Nine feet."
"Not good," Terry blurts.
"How bad—How soon?" I ask.
"When the Greenland Ice Sheet slides off,
sea level will rise thirty feet."
"How fast?" I fret.

*Atlantic Meridional Overturning Current

GREEN ICE CUBES

From my garden I pinch the tops off Sweet Basil
so it will thrive all summer till frost. As companion
plant, Basil helps tomatoes grow bigger and sweeter.
The chef across the street who harvests my mint
for desserts leaves all the Basil for me. In the blender
I add Basil to olive oil, garlic, local pecans (not
imported pine nuts). Push button to grind; tamp
and mix with chopstick; push button, repeat. Press
the mush into ice-cube trays and freeze two days.
Dump from trays into Ziplocs for winter pasta.
To save freezer space, add cheese later.

Same process: blending and freezing Jewelweed
in ice-cube trays. Gooey stem and leaf juice as
poultice prevents poison ivy rash and relieves itch
if applied fresh in the field. Hummingbirds and
honeybees pollinate the orange-yellow flowers
also called Touch Me Knot that snap shut when
touched. Quail and grouse eat the tiny seeds.
Poison ivy is virulent year round but Jewelweed
grows wild in damp ground only in summer
so freezing preserves its anti-rash gift.

In the freezer, don't confuse green ice cubes.
Do not eat Jewelweed raw. If you must,
boil it twenty minutes and change the
water twice if you want a laxative.
Smelling fresh Basil can reduce stress.

CORE SOUND MEETING

First time I rode to Beaufort with grad students
from Charlottesville, middle of the night,
we passed a sign that said, "Core Sound Meeting."
Oh good, I thought, Quakers. But in daylight
the silver historic sign said, "1731 to 1840."

The first Quakers here in 1700 were shipbuilders
from Rhode Island. William Borden built a sawmill
and shipyard at Mill Creek. The county elected
Borden to the State Legislature, but he did not serve.
A third of colonial lawmakers and Governor
Archdale were Quaker, but all left office when
forced to swear loyalty to the British king.

Borden Junior lived on Front Street in Beaufort,
now La Perla restaurant. Robert Williams built
the Hammock House and started a salt works,
evaporating seawater. In 1780, he sold his slaves.
Henry Stanton owned 1,900 acres east of Core Creek.
His great-grandson, Edwin Stanton, was Lincoln's
Secretary of War, an irony since Quakers oppose killing.

In Quaker Archives, Core Sound Meeting
eldered one woman in 1740 for gossiping and told
a man not to jump his horse so recklessly over fences.
Until 1781, Core Sound Quakers sent yearly letters
by ship to London. Opposing slavery, half of them
moved in 1840 to Ohio, Indiana; a quarter moved
to Contentnea Creek north of New Bern, and those
who stayed became Methodist—with the agreement
if Quakers came back we could have the land again.

When I moved here in 1979 and resumed
"Core Sound Meeting," Tuttles Grove Methodists
asked if local Quakers did want the land back. There
were fewer than a dozen of them, and ten of us.
Behind the church I visit the Quaker graveyard
where Borden Senior was buried in 1748.
The oldest legible stones are 1801 and 1805.
Brick-domed graves on low land may soon
flood as water rises in Newport River. Three
or five folks now attend Core Sound Meeting.

RED CLAY

Driving upstate roads,
homesick for the ocean,
I peer over bridge rails
at streams and creeks
to see if navigable
to the coast. Landlocked,
water is my compass:
blue threads on a map,
arteries across landscape
flowing downhill to salt.

After school reunion in Richmond,
from an old bridge looking east,
the James River is sunlit, running
high from last night's rainstorm.
Forty years ago, two students at UVa.
paddling the river one hot day,
Dewitt and I jumped in, floated
by our canoes, slow and lazy.

Upstream the channel is muddy brown.
A separate current from the mouth
of the Rivanna River is rusty,
eroded red clay from bare fields,
red like the soil in Monticello
gardens. Here, above where
the Rivanna meets the James—

below the steep red cliff
a new-born calf had fallen to the riverbank.
Short but strong, Dewitt lifted the calf,
climbed the bank, and I can't remember next:
Did he carry the calf to the house or
run to summon the farmer? Who said,
"Waste of time. The mother won't take
it back." "Try anyway," I said.

I haven't seen Dewitt in thirty-eight years.
Just as memories flow parallel, old friends
diverge and may never meet again.
Inland rivers end at different shores.

FIVE MISSISSIPPI

How come
thunderstorms
come at night?
In bed I wake
to drumming torrents.
Think to open
my full cisterns'
spigots.
Then kaboom,
count two elephants
and light-flash.
Wait till lightning
moves east
to flip the levers.
Five elephants
is a mile.

From every shore
in the county
I can point toward
Lookout Lighthouse
and count
fifteen elephants
until it blinks.
My three-greats
grandfather kept
a lighthouse
on the Chesapeake.

LUFF AND GUST

I am skipper of *Dorothy*, an old wooden sharpie,
in the July Fourth rally around the island.
Morning before a sailing race, I worry:
will I damage the crew, boat, or me? Two able
crew do not show. Two passengers are retired
upstate professors, come to buy beach houses.
One, recent widow, says she sailed as a child
at camp. Prediction is easy wind 10 to 12 knots,
30 percent chance of rain at noon and two.
Sailing east, the wind is light and the sails flap.
Alternately, the wind gusts to 20, and the boat
heels. I let the mainsheet slip through my hand
to spill air. Down The Cut, luff and gust. The
new crew can't comprehend port and starboard,
windward. I give clear non-nautical commands
to lean uphill, into the wind. The leeward
woman can't move. In gusts the gunnel is
an inch from capsizing. Luff and gust.

In low wind, the boat grounds on the creek beach.
I jump out to push off the sand and ask the one
more capable to hold the tiller "toward the houses,"
straight north, until I can haul myself back aboard.
More than she can handle. Broken hip four years ago,
I'm not so nimble myself. I cannot rely on any help
from these two. If we sail away from protection
of the land, the wind will blow more than 20 knots.
Out in North River, I watch Gini and Roger reef
their sail. Whitecaps are boiling, water is steely gray.

The sky is ugly black to the south, east and west.
I decide to turn back west to the Museum dock.
Better part of valor. Two sailboats follow me. We
tie up, drinking beer and cider at the Finz deck
until the fleet returns, four of five boats damaged.
Vic's boat capsized. Brent cracked his mast-step.
One boat is towed back with a busted rudder.
Another a torn sail. In Back Sound on a sandbar
in front of Carrot Island, the wind gusted to 45.
Hail the size of quarters. I feel smug, having
returned the Museum boat *Dorothy* unscathed.
I saw danger and turned back.

MY MOTHER CALLED ME "DOLL"

From my mother's mother I inherited a china-head doll.
My "Granny" doll wears a calico dress, blue velvet sash,
lace collar and cuffs, eyelet petticoat and pantaloons.
White skin, rouged cheeks, blue eyes and tight black curls.

Just like Granny Smith, age twenty, leaning her bicycle
by the gazebo at the Rose Garden in Hartford where
her father Paddy Horan was gardener. In that Sunday
photo (June 4, 1899, scribbled in pencil), right before
she married Clarence Smith, an Irishman who would
be elected judge, she wore a long black skirt, white
shirtwaist, butterfly pin at her neck. Boater straw hat
by her gloves on the bench. Tiny waist and big bust,
figure like my mother's picture at the same age.
Smiling eyes, strong chin and round cheeks, the girl
in this faded photo, for me like looking in a mirror.

By the time she was thirty-five, Granny had white
hair and ten children, my mother the youngest.
At my parents' wedding, Granny Smith was short
and stout, waist as wide as her shoulders. She wore
black laced shoes, a string of minks. Granny Smith died
before I was one year old. At the beach, I heard she sat
prim, fully dressed, under an umbrella and once fell
into the river stepping from a dock to a boat. A cousin
said she slapped him when he ran across the street
to play with lower-caste neighbors. Like my mother
on and off all my life, at sixty Granny spent six months
in a psychiatric hospital for a rest cure. But not me,
not yet. More sporty, I'm half her girth. Till sixty,
like my father, my hair is dark as the china doll's.
Yet looking at Granny's face, I see my own eyes.

PERSEVERANCE

Fishing near Asheville, a rock collector saw black sands
of corundum, the mother mineral of blue sapphires and
red rubies. Three years, he dug eight feet deep to unearth
four big star rubies, hard as diamonds, a thousand
times rarer than rubies. He said, *"When I found them,
a red-tailed hawk soared right over me."* Thirty years later,
the pigeon-blood stones are being auctioned in New York
for ninety million dollars to benefit his widow. The four
total 342 carats. How big are they? Apples? Grapefruit?

After digging several days, I find my star ruby ring
in a silk bag stashed in a drawer thirty-five years.
The setting is smooth so facets wouldn't snag when
I was pulling fish from gill nets or weaving wool.
Who was I half my life ago— before divorce?
I have moved back into the Beaufort house I paid for.
I can just as well wear a wedding ring I paid for.

By showing a ring on my left hand, where it fits,
I don't want to discourage a gentle man's approach,
so I have it made bigger to wear on my right. One carat
feels heavy. When I asked about my potential, a professor
once told me, *"My dear, all you need is persev'erance."* Like
purple stones that wait eons underground for light to refract.

NEW BRIDGE RANT

In Beaufort, we are fond of our old drawbridge. You don't
toss out old shoes, old dogs, or old men that still work.
We fought a new high bridge twenty years. The fixed span
will block historic tall-ships from the Museum Dock, tall
masts from hiding in hurricane holes, and block big-boat
repairs at Jarrett Bay, the county's biggest employer.
The State says it wants to improve access to develop
Downeast. or does it want to speed trucks to the Port?

Already high tide fills ditches the level of Downeast roads
and floods the highway across the Wildlife Refuge
to Cedar Island. Money better spent to fix our potholes,
raise low creek crossings. If a Hurricane like Fran hits
Beaufort, says Rick Luettich, who predicted Katrina
would breach New Orleans levees, we can't evacuate:
Highway 101 will be underwater for six miles.

NC DOT paid 70 million dollars to a New Jersey company,
not even local flagmen. Why not build seven ten-million-
dollar bridges we need? Five years, and they're not done.
Why not ten seven-million-dollar bridges? Pile-drivers
thump for two years, booming deep in our guts and
scaring away our dear dolphins, damaging delicate sonar.
Rumor is pilings sunk in the marsh are already cracking,
not dug deep enough. I hear the two bridge halves, west
to east, do not meet in the middle. The colossal arch blocks
our sunset and obstructs training water for Junior Sailing.
During construction, no one can navigate the detours. Where
the Downeast Bypass dumps at Olga Road on Highway 70,
there are accidents every day. When two of four lanes
finally open, traffic backs up an hour, so they allow us
to cross our old drawbridge again for one more month.

I hope the bridge engineers are wiser than their landscapers
who advise Bradford Pears to line the "approach" to Beaufort.
These weak trees bloom frothy white one week a year.
Petals blow off like snow in the Back Street parking lot, when
the wind blows 50 miles an hour three days straight in the
hottest February ever. Trees might last fifteen or twenty years.
Wind cracks their brittle branches and upends shallow roots,
and the wind does tend to blow at the coast. Not great for trees
to fall down by our escape route. Go to a plant nursery.
Ask if they sell Bradford Pears, and if they say yes. Leave.

STEERING *HALCYON*

The land is dearer for the sea, the ocean for the shore
LUCY LARCOM

First two weeks of January are zero wind-chill at dawn.
At an icy oyster roast, Shawn, schooner captain aboard
75-foot *Halcyon* at the Beaufort Dock, shares a video
of his daughter winning a swimming race in Maine.
Homesick, he's patching deck leaks middle of the night.
"Beaufort is better for boat repairs than Lauderdale,"
he says. A mechanic overhauls engines on the boat.
Best Buy Geeks rig new computers, radios, TVs.
George the canvas-man tailors fifty new cushions.
When Shawn's young crew arrive, I feed them dinner.
All a foot taller than me and decades younger,
they trust me since I used to deliver sailboats.

I've given up ocean sailing, but when the acrobatic crew
bend a new mainsail on *Halcyon*'s 100-foot mast and
tweak the rigging to get rid of wrinkles, I stand at the helm.
Hoisting the mainsail, Justin tends the halyard, Shawn
the clew outhaul on the boom, Margaret the sheets.
Grin on my face, I grip the wheel that comes to my chest.
Local knowledge, I steer out the Inlet, inside channel markers
until deep enough I can fall off toward the Lighthouse.
Margaret the mate drops the centerboard, drawing 14 feet.
Justin the chef and engineer bakes us pastries.

> *Tickled, I am sailing. I can still do this.*
"Full and by," says Captain Shawn, so I hold my course,
190 degrees. I can easily wrangle 16 knots of wind, sunny
morning late January. Two dolphins tumble in our wake.
Two wide-wingspan gannets, open-ocean seabirds, fly bow high.
Benison. I want to keep sailing to the Islands.
> *I can still do this. I could even fall in love again.*

Halcyon must delay three more days in port
for repairs, more parts and food to provision.
Temperature drops again. Big wind 40-plus knots
predicted offshore, 20-foot-plus seas like I sailed
thirty years ago. But the boat must leave to meet
the rich Texas owner in Guadeloupe. I help lift
the dinghy to the foredeck, but its outboard engine
would crush the hull. They will tow it and must cut it
loose, when it fills with water. Wish I had asked
that they give the dinghy to Junior Sailing.

      I could go, but choose to stay home, warm safe and dry.
Ten days, I scan bad weather on windy[dot]com
and daily emails from Shawn's wife of their position:
due east to Bermuda as possible bail-point, then
due south for wind angle. They do cut loose the dinghy.
My comfort: *Halcyon*, ancients called the kingfisher
who makes a floating nest on the Aegean Sea.
Ovid believed she can calm the wind and waves
around her while brooding her eggs.

DESCANT

1

At New Years, wise Bess wrote me that she is
losing her memory. Jim Murray, my biology professor,
had brought Bess back from Oxford to Virginia. On
botany field trips at Mountain Lake forty years ago,
from Bess I learned to say plant names in British.
She pronounced lilies—*FRItillaries* and the orange
butterfly—*FriTILLary.* Department chair, lanky Jim
was more formal. No less clever, lean blond Bess
in overalls shot the fox that messed with her chickens.

I have always wanted to grow up like the Murrays—
naturalists and wilderness defenders, dinner debates
instead of television. When they climbed mountains
around the world, I tended her dogs, asparagus, cows,
chickens. They had never quite finished remodeling
their 200-year-old brick house, raising three children,
all now professors too, who nursed me after surgery
when I crushed my wrist, and Bess administered
Demerol painkiller, same drug that killed Elvis.

2

In March sun, on her porch above Bentivar pond,
Bess recalls my surgery thirty-eight years ago better
than today. While she rests, Jim and I walk by the pond,
red-clay gardens, the Rivanna floodplain. Up the lane,
he says, "She sleeps a lot." No apparent cause or cure.

After Jim has shared his sadness, he slips
along the spring-green bottom to check his
young chestnut trees. In the creek, Purple-Blue!
floating in the weir of stepping-stones, the size
of thumbnails. I reach under the butterfly, not to
pinch wing dust. Place it atop a fencepost to dry.
The proboscis twitches. Wings wiggle a smidge.
Just the wind? I learned from the Murrays
to pay attention. Spring Azure blows to the back
of my crooked wrist. And pops up!

3

Back on the Carolina coast, *Tradescantia* is blooming—
blue-purple, three petals the thumbnail size
of the Bentivar butterfly. Rich word for spiderwort.
I enunciate the botanic species, *virginiana*, like Bess.
Plant explorers, John Tradescant Father and Son,
Kings' Gardeners, stored their rare plants in
Oxford's Ashmolean. Some may call wild, unruly
Tradescantia a weed. Sturdy stalks outside my gardens
bloom March to November, keeping Bess alive:
Blue-purple petals like wings. I am not ready to lose
wry Bess, best mentor, or become an elder yet myself.
When I hear Bess has died, by my well-pump
out back, one spiderwort blooms white.

HURRICANE,
BEAUFORT SCALE FORCE 12

1

In a hurricane, there are two choices: to stay or to leave. Two
horrors: Waiting in my house in wind & rain & dark, wondering
if the roof and windows will hold on. Or, evacuating to Virginia
and watching from distance as Florence approaches offshore as
Category 4 and 5. She wreaks havoc as only Cat 2 and not a direct
hit—12-foot storm surge, wind 110 miles per hour stalled four days,
30 inches of rain. Saltwater floods hundreds of houses in the county;
tornadoes shred ten friends' roofs. Trees take down power lines. No
lights in Beaufort for eight days; none Downeast ten days. Electric
linemen are heroes. Driving back, I hit the lucky, narrow window
between power back on and highway bridges closed from upstate
rivers cresting. Away and back, I re-fill gas every quarter tank.

Storm surge crushed docks, flooded downtown shops, left debris
high on Front Street lawns. Most everyone says, when asked,
"It could have been much worse." A dozen pecan trees I know
fell down or lost half their branches. Sailboats from the creek,
blown, lifted onto Bird Shoal. All wild horses on the islands
survive the wind and surge; we hope our shorebirds endure.
Friend Bev in Montana calls again: "How much longer are you
going to live near hurricanes?" I'm not moving anytime soon.
My lifework is clean water: in it on it, looking at it.

2

The spirit of neighbors helping neighbors lifts our hearts.
Beaufort Grocery serves free meals for a week from Benjy's
food truck. Ann Street Methodist disperses bottled water,
canned food, Clorox, buckets, diapers, tarps—organized by
Julia Royall, youth pastor in shorts and tattoos. Pet Provisions
sends free dog and cat food across the county. Taylor McCune's
Facebook keeps us all informed. Three gentlemen with chainsaws
and red tractor-with-a-lift cut branches; three of us follow, hauling
debris to the street. In my dog Kiwi's backyard so she'll be safe,
I lop and drag branches, rake sixteen bags of leaves then mow so
grass will grow again. My house is fine, four shingles blown off
and not leaking yet. A blown limb knocked twenty shingles off
my Shed roof, and rain fell neatly into a stashed canoe in the garage
—at first glance; then when I take time after five days, I find water
in every bucket and box of boat and bike parts and rusting tools,
and a month later I see a rafter about to crack and crash. To toss
thawed shrimp and squid bait from a neighbor's freezer, I should
have worn a HazMat suit. The only way I can clean ice slush in
my own freezer, after two weeks volunteering, is pretend I am
helping someone else. Not foul because, before evacuating,
I moved out fish and left frozen half-gallons of water. I make
jam from thawed blueberries for chainsaw crew and friends
who lost houses. When Piggly Wiggly stocks their freezer again,
I hand out Klondike Bars to roofers, cops, trash collectors.

3

The third horror of a hurricane is the "ubiquitous toxicity"[1] of
the aftermath. Apartments with black mold are evicting tenants
who have no place to go. Flooding rivers upstate carry to coastal
estuaries a million dead chickens, pathogens[2] from overflowing hog
lagoons and human sewage, heavy metals[3] in Duke Power coal-ash
—the State Legislature having gutted regulations. Liveaboards
on sailboats in the creek tell me they have rash on their hands.
I won't let Kiwi swim at Radio Island, and I won't kayak or eat
seafood, for another month, at least. Mosquitoes the size of
wasps multiply in standing water. The County aerial sprays
Monsanto mosquito-poison that kills larval oysters, clams,
and fish on waters where commercial fishermen earn a living.
Imagine the ghastly catastrophe if the Feds permit offshore
oil-rigs so storm surge can dump oil sludge[4] on our beaches
and homes, kill birds and fish. What about our dolphins?

---

1 Jedidiah Purdy, *After Nature, A Politics for the Anthropocene*
2 Hog waste viruses and bacteria include E. coli, salmonella, giardia, crypto-
  sporidium, toxoplasma, campylobacter, hepatitis.
3 Coal ash heavy metals include arsenic, lead, mercury, cadmium, chromium,
  zinc, manganese, vanadium, selenium, molybdenum, nickel, iron, beryllium.
4 Oil contains volatile organic compounds like benzene that cause cancer
  and polycyclic aromatic hydrocarbons. Dispersants are more toxic than oil.

4

I try to mitigate horror with redemption. Neighbors
helping neighbors. Purple flowers blooming in my garden
are Mexican petunia, sage, aster. I plant daffodil bulbs and
rosemary; kale, chard, arugula; and a tiny pecan tree out back.
Third week after Florence landed, apple, cherry, and pear trees,
having lost so many leaves, are blooming because they think
it is spring. Still ninety degrees in October, but power for a/c
is on. And there are no more paid-parking meters downtown.
From the high bridge, I see a double rainbow, red-orange-yellow-
green-blue-indigo-violet, grounded in Pine Knoll Shores and
Mill Creek. My brother says it's a promise of no more flooding.

MIRABILE DICTU

Inside I feel the pull of tides—sensing
high and low, like the periwinkle snail
that climbs Spartina on each tide cycle.
Ignore deadlines on my desk:

The sky is blue. With lucky timing,
wind and tide at my back push me paddling
six miles around Carrot Island. Overhead
wheeling gulls and terns, pelicans in formation.

The tidal current streams east out Taylors Creek.
Sunday morning no motorboat wake. On the shore,
Louisiana heron, burnished osprey on a bush.
Slack high at Lennoxville Point's eroding bank.

Kingfishers chitter from fallen-tree branches.
Northeast breeze blows me out North River into
the sound by copper-green Middle Marsh to island
hammocks where white ibis and egrets stand sentinel.

Abnormally high tide, I can float over mudflat
channels usually dry, as the Sargasso Sea,
offshore, slumps a bit because Arctic ice melt
slows the Gulf Stream flowing north by Iceland.

Four inches of rain in one day floods Front Street.
Worst year ever for pollen, mosquitoes, fleas. Hottest
August and September on record, ocean 70 degrees
in November. Don't fret sea level. Today, see abundance:

Summer plovers and sandpipers still here, winter birds
arriving. On a shoal, watch fall migrants: among still
whimbrels, two gamboling godwits on their way to
Patagonia, whose long bills curve upward "toward God."

Acknowledgments

"2015/ 1970/ 1670" and "How to Survive a Bee Attack" appeared in
   NC Literary Review, both Finalists, James Applewhite Prize
"Rowing Forward, Facing Backward" in *Tar River Poetry*
"Green Thought in Green Shade" in *Literary Trails of Eastern NC:
   A Guidebook*
"Such Grace," "Twilight" as "Créspuscule," "Rowing Forward, Facing
   Backward," "Dwell in Safety," "Swimming in a Meteor Shower,"
   "Green Thought in Green Shade," "Mirabile Dictu" (all revised)
   in *Salt Runs in My Blood* (Kakapo Press)

Thanks for residencies at Virginia Center for the Creative Arts
at Sweet Briar and Auvillar, France; Bread Loaf, Vermont Studio
Center, and a Cape Cod Dune Shack. And for fellowships from
American Association of University Women, National Science
Foundation, National Endowment for the Arts, Fulbright, and
North Carolina Arts Council. I have learned about craft from writers in workshops I took and taught. Gratitude to my Beaufort Writing Group and Cru Poets critique community.

About the Author

As developmental editor, **SUSAN SCHMIDT** polishes science and history books, novels, and memoirs—listed among Top Ten Editors in New England. She has been a professor of literature and environmental decision-making, and a government science-policy analyst. She has had a Coast Guard Captain's license thirty-six years. She wrote the grant to buy Carrot Island and Bird Shoal in Beaufort for the NC Estuarine Reserve. She has a doctorate in American literature and Masters degrees in Environmental Sciences and British lit. She read literature at Oxford and, postdoc, studied bioethics and environmental mediation.

To witness natural diversity, she walked the Camino de Santiago, Cornwall Coastal Path, Scottish Highlands, Ireland's Ring of Kerry, Snowdonia in Wales, Guernsey and Brittany, and the Appalachian Trail. She surveyed birds in Kenya, Ecuador, Belize, and Iceland; paddled Alaska's Prince William Sound and New Zealand's Milford Sound; and delivered sailboats to the West Indies. Her homeplace is the Chesapeake Bay in Virginia, and her homeport is Beaufort, North Carolina, where she walks beaches with her Boykin Spaniel.

Her poems won the Guy Owen Poetry Prize and appear in *Literary Trails of Eastern North Carolina*; two poems were finalists for the James Applewhite Prize. She wrote *Landfall Along the Chesapeake, In the Wake of Captain John Smith*, an ecological history and boat adventure; *Song of Moving Water*, a novel about a young woman who organizes her community to oppose a dam; and *Salt Runs in My Blood*, poems about fish, birds, playing in boats, and walking long trails.

susu@susanschmidt.net
www.susanschmidt.net

Made in the USA
Columbia, SC
20 November 2018